Date Due

2-1-75			

KEEPING TIME

KEEPING
TIME

Written and Illustrated By

Walter Buehr

G. P. Putnam's Sons   New York

Other Books by Walter Buehr

Through the Locks: Canals Today and Yesterday
Treasure: The Story of Money and Its Safeguarding
Harbors and Cargoes
Ships of the Great Lakes
Trucks and Trucking
Knights and Castles and Feudal Life
Railroads Today and Yesterday
Cargoes in the Sky
The Crusaders
Sending the Word: The Story of Communication
The Genie and the Word: Electricity and Communication

Illustrations and Text
© 1960 by Walter Buehr
All rights reserved.

Published simultaneously in the Dominion of Canada
by Longmans, Green and Company

Library of Congress Catalog Card Number: 60-6863
MANUFACTURED IN THE UNITED STATES OF AMERICA

Contents

To Everett

KEEPING TIME

1. The Calendar

LONG, long ago, when our cave-men forefathers were hunting their game with clubs and stones and afterward eating it raw, time was very simple. It was either day or night. There were no trains to catch, classes to be on time for, TV programs to turn on or dinner hours to remember. You just had to be sure to get back to your cave before it got dark enough for a saber-toothed tiger to ambush you.

Today, time enters into everything we do. In a world where almost nothing seems sure or secure, most of us feel that good old Time is the one thing that never varies. We believe that the sun and moon will rise and set right on schedule, that the seasons will follow each other in perfect order, and that the calendar couldn't possibly be in error.

Well, the astronomers tell us that our great solar system is full of little slips and wobbles, which have puzzled them for centuries. It has caused endless confusion to those who have been trying to measure time and design calendars.

Once people used to think that the sun came up from out of a great sea, to the east, a sea which encircled the earth, and then set in the waters to the west. They believed that the earth, shaped like a giant dinner plate, was the center of the universe, and that the sun, moon and stars were small heavenly bodies hung from under a dome-shaped heaven.

Now we all know that our earth is like a slightly out-of-shape ball and it is only a small, very unimportant, dot in the great universe. We know that the sun doesn't move but that our earth orbits around the sun once a year, at the same time spinning on its own axis every twenty-four hours. When our part of the earth faces the sun it is day; when it is turned away we have darkness.

This sounds very nice and orderly, doesn't it? Then we learn that the earth doesn't travel around the sun in a circular orbit, but rather in an ellipse, or oval. Its pace is not absolutely even — it moves faster at certain times than at others. It doesn't rotate smoothly on its axis but has a slight wobble. It doesn't even make its daily orbit in the same length of time but sometimes is a little slow or fast. Therefore the solar day, measured by the time it takes the sun to reach a certain meridian which it left the day before, isn't always exactly the same.

Our forefathers were a long time discovering how to correct those little celestial mistakes. They knew that their calendars were going wrong when they realized that the equinoxes and the solstices didn't fall on the same dates each year but were occurring a little earlier or later, according to their particular way of reckoning.

Let's make sure that *we* know what equinoxes and solstices are, before we go any further. The earth, in its yearly trip around the sun, tilts slowly, first to the south and then to the north, while still spinning around once every day. By June 21st it has reached its greatest tilt to the south, so the sun seems to be passing overhead farthest north of the equator, on its daily journey. This is the summer solstice, when days are longest in the Northern Hemisphere (the half of the earth north of the equator) because the tilt lets us see the sun longest.

On December 21st the opposite tilt is greatest; this is the winter solstice, and the shortest day of the year in the Northern Hemisphere, because the curvature of the earth lets us see less of the sun between sunrise and sunset. In the Southern Hemisphere just the opposite takes place. In Argentina or Chile it is winter in June and summer in December.

Halfway between the solstices the sun makes its daily passage from sunrise to sunset directly above the equator twice each year. The passage on March 21st is called the vernal equinox, that on September 21st is the autumnal equinox.

The equinoxes and solstices mark the seasons. Winter begins on December 21st, the winter solstice, and lasts until the vernal equinox on March 21st. Spring begins then and lasts until June 21st, the summer solstice, and is followed by summer, which runs to September 21st. Autumn begins on that day, the autumnal equinox, and continues to December 21st.

This can be much more easily understood if you can find a globe map of the world, which also contains an analemma or diagram of the sun's path from solstice to solstice.

The word "month" comes from "moon," and we divide the year into twelve months because the moon revolves around the earth twelve times a year, once about every 28 days. The names of the months came from the Romans, who began their ten-month year with March. At first their months were numbered; our present September came from the Roman *septem* (7), October from *octo* (8), November from *novem* (9) and December from *decem* (10).

Later our first month, January, came from Janus, the Roman two-faced God of beginnings and endings. February came from the Roman Februa, a feast of purification, while March was named after Mars, the God of War. April stems from either *apero* or *afar*, two ancient words meaning "latter" or "second." May was named for Maia, Goddess of Increase, and June for Junius, a Roman family name.

Julius Caesar, besides being a great military leader and lawgiver, also tried his hand at measuring time. He started the ten-month Julian calendar on January 1, 45 B.C. To make it start properly, the previous year had to have 445 days. It was known as the Year of Confusion, and no wonder.

Caesar changed the name of our present seventh month to Julius, after himself. This became July in English. When Augustus became Emperor of Rome he also wanted a month named in his honor, so he changed Sextilius (6th) to August. It had only 30 days, and Augustus wasn't going to allow any month named after him to be shorter than a 31-day Julius, so he stole a day from February and added it to August.

By 1582 the Julian calendar was so far off that the

15

vernal equinox, which should have fallen on March 21st, occurred on March 11th. A more accurate calendar would just have to be worked out soon. Pope Gregory set his astronomers and mathematicians to the task of figuring out a new and more correct one, and later that year the Pope by Papal Bull or edict proclaimed a new calendar, which was later called the Gregorian calendar. It contained twelve months, five of them 30 days long, six of 31 days and one, February, of 28 days, totaling a 365-day year.

This was still not quite long enough, because a sidereal year, which is measured by observation of the stars and is the most accurate method of measuring time, is 365 days, 6 hours and 9 minutes long. Therefore the slack of those extra hours was taken up by declaring an extra day in February every four years, which they called "leap year." This almost balanced the sidereal and calendar year. There is still a tiny error of 26 seconds a year in the Gregorian calendar, but it seems to be the most accurate calendar man can devise.

Unfortunately, 1582 was a bad year to get the Protestant countries like England to agree to anything a Catholic Pope backed. Bitter warfare between Catholics and Protestants was raging in Europe and no agreement would be possible between them for a long time.

Not until 1752, almost two hundred years later, did England and the other Protestant countries finally adopt the Gregorian calendar. When the change-over was made, eleven days had to be dropped from the 1752 calendar. The common people of that time had very little education, so when they were told that they would lose eleven days, many thought that their lives were being shortened by that much. For days crowds rioted in the cities, demanding their eleven days back.

While the Jews and Chinese still reckon time by ancient calendars of their own, only once has a new calendar been adopted since 1752. That was during the French Revolution, in 1792. Then the new revolutionary government proclaimed a new one, with different names for the days of the week and the months. After the revolution this was abandoned and the Gregorian calendar has remained the standard for most of the world.

2. Measuring The Hours

SO much for calendar time. Now let's look at the problem of measuring the hours of the day. When we talk of a "day," we usually mean the true or apparent solar day — the actual time it takes the sun to make a circuit of the earth, from any meridian of longitude back to that same meridian, about 24 hours later.

Astronomers discovered long ago that the rotation of the earth varies a little in speed from day to day. Therefore it was impossible to make absolutely accurate time observations from the *sun* to find the length of a day. The best that could be done was to take an average over the year, which was called the "mean solar day." This is 24 hours, 3 minutes and 56.5 seconds long.

For accurate observations astronomers observe the

orbits of the stars. Their wobbles and errors don't change the calculations enough to matter because the stars are so far away. Now let's find out how the astronomers do their work at such important and famous observatories as those in Greenwich, England, and our own Arlington, Virginia.

A star is "timed" as it passes over the meridian on which the observatory lies. The meridian is an imaginary line in the sky, passing through the zenith and the north and south points. The instrument used to determine time is a meridian transit telescope. This is pivoted so that it can be pointed anywhere along the meridian, but nowhere else. When the viewer sees a star appear in the scope he moves a slender perpendicular wire across the lens of the scope. When the star crosses the wire an electrical contact is made, which is registered on a chronograph or cylindrical drum covered with paper. When the star crosses the wire, closing the circuit, small dents are made in the paper. A sidereal clock in a sealed glass case also registers smaller dents on the paper. The two sets of dents are then compared, thus checking the accuracy of the clock.

Even more accurate is an instrument called the "photographic zenith tube." This is a telescope which is rigidly fixed so that it can only photograph stars which pass very near the zenith. At the lower end of the tube is a basin filled with mercury. When a star appears near the zenith its light passes through a lens at the upper end of the scope, goes down the tube, is reflected from the surface of the mercury and is focused on a small photographic plate just under the lens. The time when the photograph is taken is the star's meridian transit, the exact split second when the star has crossed the meridian.

If you'd like to tell time from the stars yourself, here is a simple but very interesting experiment you can do right at home. All you need is a clear, dark night, a pencil and paper and a simple formula.

Go outdoors where you can see the North or Pole Star and the Big Dipper, which almost everybody recognizes. The Pole Star is the brightest star you come to if you follow upward a line through the two stars which form the side of the Dipper opposite the handle side.

Now think of the Pole Star as the center of a clock face, with 12 straight overhead and 6 straight down. Then imagine those two stars of the Dipper, Alpha and Beta, as forming the outer end of an hour hand which is pivoted on the Pole Star. Call this hour hand AB.

Now observe where the imaginary hour hand

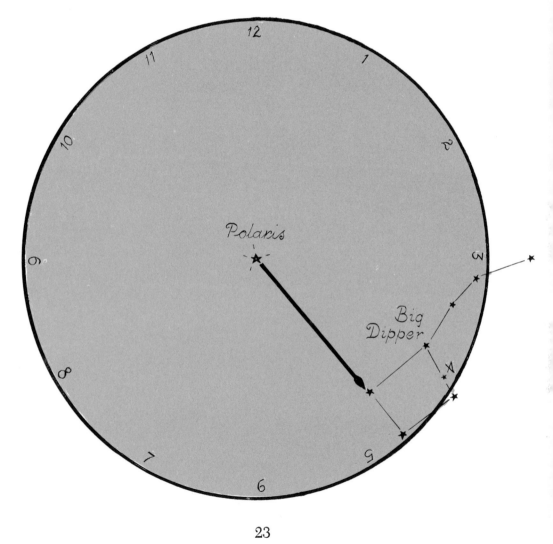

Polaris

Big
Dipper

12
11
10
9
8
7
6
5
4
3
2
1

23

touches the circle of imaginary numbers around the face of the clock. Remember if 12 is straight up, 3 would be halfway down on the right side and 9 halfway down on the left — just like a real clock. Write down the time shown by the end of the hour hand AB on the sky clock, and call it TD. Call the number of months from January to the first of the present month M, and the date today DM. Here is the formula:

1. (TD plus M) x 2 = X hrs. and X min.
2.   DM x 4   = X min.
3.   Add = X hrs. and X min.
   Subtract this sum from (4 hrs. 15 min.). If the sum is too large to subtract keep adding multiples of 12 hours to (4 hrs. 15 min.) until this is larger than the first sum, so you *can* subtract.
4. The result is star time for your position in longitude.

For example:

On the evening of November 25th you have observed the imaginary hour hand pointing a little to the right of the bottom of the sky clock, and decided it said 4:24 P.M. November is the 11th month so M will be 10.

$$\text{TD} \quad 4:24$$
$$\underline{\text{M} \quad 10:00}$$
$$14:24 \text{ x } 2 = 28 \text{ hrs. } 48 \text{ min.}$$

(Nov. 25th) DM 25 x 4 = 100 min. $= \underline{\quad 1 \text{ hr. } \quad 40 \text{ min.}}$

$$30 \text{ hrs. } 28 \text{ min.}$$

Now subtract (30 hrs. 28 min.) from (4 hrs. 15 min.) which you can't do without adding three multiples of 12, or 36, which makes

$$4 \text{ hrs. } 15 \text{ min.}$$
$$\underline{36 \text{ hrs.}}$$
$$40 \text{ hrs. } 15 \text{ min.}$$

Now you can subtract:

$$40 \text{ hrs. } 15 \text{ min.}$$
$$\underline{30 \text{ hrs. } 28 \text{ min.}}$$
$$9 \text{ hrs. } 47 \text{ min.}$$

This gives you local star time for your exact position in longitude, or 9:47 P.M.

If you want to correct star time to zone time, which is the time of your living-room clock, you must subtract 8½ minutes for each hundred miles your home lies west of your time zone meridian. You can find the zone meridians on the zone map in this book. If you have read your sky clock hand right, you'll get a result within 3 or 4 minutes of your living-room clock.

Did you know that the sun can be your compass if you are lost in the woods? You will never circle endlessly as most people do when they are lost, if you carry a watch and the sun is shining.

Simply hold your watch up so that the hour hand points directly at the sun. Then south will be halfway between the hour hand and 12 on your watch dial, measuring forward the way the hands move if it is morning, and backward in the afternoon.

A modern solar day begins at midnight and ends at the next midnight, at a time when the sun is shining on the opposite side of the earth. In ancient times days were measured differently. The Greeks' day started at sunrise and ended at sunset; this period was divided into 12 equal parts or "hours," but since the daylight day is always getting longer and shorter, the Greek hour was never the same length on any two days. Imagine the figuring it would take to set your alarm clock to wake you at the same time every morning! We don't know what the Greeks did about keeping time at night — maybe they all went to bed with the chickens.

When the early astronomers discovered that the earth wasn't really flat like a plate but globe-shaped, they had to change their whole system of mapping the earth. They couldn't use straight lines intersecting to make squares in which to locate geographical points because the surface of the earth was curved. Therefore they drew two sets of imaginary lines at right angles to each other. One was a series of circles parallel to each other and equally distant. They started from the equator (a circle halfway between the two poles) which they called "0 latitude," and went to each pole, at 90 degrees latitude. They were called "parallels of latitude," and the distance between two degrees was 60 nautical miles.

Crossing these circles of latitude at right angles they drew another set of lines encircling the earth from north to south and passing through the North and South poles. There were 24 of them, 15 degrees apart, and they were named "meridians of longitude." Each degree of longitude was divided into 60 minutes (of distance, not time). At the equator where the earth's diameter is greatest and the meridians were farthest apart, each minute of longitude equaled one mile. But to make the division come out even, the astronomers needed a unit a little longer than the existing land mile, so they adopted the nautical mile for measurements at sea. The nautical mile equals 1⅛ land miles.

Now with the earth neatly divided into segments by the crisscrossing lines of longitude and latitude, the map makers could locate any place on earth exactly, and make up tables showing the altitude or height above the horizon of any heavenly body, seen from any place in the world at any hour of any day.

For instance, tables in their nautical almanac showed on which parallel of latitude the sun appeared to cross from east to west on each day of the year. This was known as the sun's "declination." By measuring the height of the sun above the horizon at its zenith (at noon) it was a simple to figure its latitude for that day. Other tables showed that when it was high noon at Greenwich, England (when the sun was over 0 longitude), it would be 6 A.M. anywhere on the 90th degree, west longitude, because it would take the sun six hours to appear above that meridian. At that same instant it would be 6 P.M. at 90 degrees *east* longitude because the sun had already passed over that meridian 6 hours before. At all places on the 180th degree, on the other side of the earth from Greenwich, it would be midnight.

Now what about places that lay between the meridians? If your town A was 120 miles west of another town B located directly on a meridian, the sun would pass over you about ten minutes after it had passed over B. If you both set your clocks by the sun, it would be noon at B ten minutes earlier. This was called "local time," and until 1883 all time was local time.

This was because there was no quick way to transmit time signals from some central point for long distances. There was as yet no telegraph, telephone or radio, so clocks could only be corrected by the sun. Still, since nobody could travel faster than the pace of a horse or sailing ship, differences of ten or twenty minutes within a few miles didn't matter.

Then the world began to speed up. With the spread of railroads, steamship lines and the telegraph, distances shrank and trouble started. Imagine how hard it must have been for a railroad to try to print a time-table when the clocks of each station on the line were set to a different local time. Nobody knew when a train was due to arrive or depart and no two watches seemed to agree.

This confusion continued until instant signals could be flashed by wire from a central observatory all over the land. Then the world was organized into a series of time zones, each one 15 degrees of longitude wide. This was started in the United States, on Sunday, November 18, 1883, mostly through the efforts of the railroads. There was no law enforcing the time change for many years.

Within each zone all the clocks were set to the time of that zone, regardless of whether they were at the eastern, middle or western side of the zone. In the United States except for Hawaii and Alaska, there are four zones: Eastern, from 75 to 90 degrees, west longitude; Central from 90 to 105 degrees; Mountain,

from 105 degrees to 120 degrees; and Pacific from 120 degrees to the coast. The zones don't always follow the meridians. Where a zone line would divide a town into two zones, it zigzags to avoid such confusion.

Travelers passing from one zone to another, westward, must set their watches one hour earlier at each crossing. When they go east they lose an hour each time.

The establishment of these time zones cleared up the confusion over hourly time, but there still remained the question of where to begin one day and end the preceding one. At some meridian on the globe one 24-hour day would have to end and a new day begin. Any meridian would do as far as keeping time was concerned, but imagine the confusion that would follow if the line at 75 degrees west longitude were chosen. This line runs just east of Philadelphia, so it would still be Sunday in that city, Baltimore and Washington while it had become Monday in New York and Boston. A salesman leaving New York on a Monday morning train would find the office in Philadelphia he meant to call on, closed because it was still Sunday there. A Baltimore man leaving home Saturday night to spend Sunday with a relative in Boston would arrive there just in time to meet his cousin leaving his home for work on Monday morning.

The astronomers therefore located their interna-

Time Zones

tional date line along a meridian where it would cause the least confusion. They chose the 180th degree, because that meridian runs through the lonely Pacific from the Arctic to the Antarctic without touching land except for a small tip of Siberia and a few Pacific islands. To avoid having the line touch even these sparsely inhabited places they zigzagged it to run down the middle of the Bering Straits and around the island groups. Therefore you can only go through the strange experience of having two Sundays in two days or of going to sleep at one A.M. Monday morning and waking up after a good night's sleep at nine A.M. on *Sunday,* by being aboard a ship or plane crossing the Pacific.

Modern plane design is rapidly approaching the time when air liners will move faster than the sun, which whizzes over us at 900 miles an hour. In fact some of our military planes already beat that speed. When the air liners do, a passenger will be able to board a plane in New York after a nine o'clock breakfast, and arrive in San Francisco before he leaves New York — at least he will according to California clocks. When he arrives he will be in plenty of time for another nine o'clock breakfast with his San Francisco friends. Won't it be an odd sensation, to look backward from a westbound 1000-mile-an-hour plane and watch the morning sun slowly setting in the *east!*

Sun Dial

Sand or
Hour Glass

3. Mechanical Timekeepers

EVEN in ancient times astronomers had observed
the movements of the sun, moon and stars, and
so were able to figure out calendars and keep track of
the seasons. What baffled them most for centuries was
the problem of measuring the hours of the day and
night accurately.

Water Clock

Candle Clock

Nobody knows who built the first device for measuring time, or even what kind of a contrivance it was. We do know that the ancient Egyptians and Greeks did have several kinds of clocks.

Probably the earliest and simplest timekeeper was the sundial. This device tells time by the movement of its own shadow across a flat surface marked with the hours of daylight. Perhaps some prehistoric man noticed how the shadow from a tree trunk crawled across the sand in front of his cave, day after day at almost the same time. Then it occurred to him to use the shadow to time the happenings of his daily life.

He might tell his wife he'd be back from the hunt when the shadow in front of the cave touched the cliff edge, and to be sure to have a hot chunk of broiled mastodon ready.

Finally people began to build sundials marked with hours of equal length. Then they discovered that the shadow made by the sun changed a little every day with the changing seasons, which changed the lengths of the hours. To correct this error they set the gnomen (the upright part of the sundial which cast the shadow) over a concave surface like the inside of a bowl. The curved insides of the bowl corrected the changes in the shadow caused by the sun's declination, provided the lines marking the hours were correctly curved too.

Such sundials were very expensive because it took a lot of figuring and careful work to make them. Then it was discovered that if the gnomen of a sundial is tilted to one side so that it points directly at the North Star, the gnomen's shadow won't change with the seasons. That made a sundial much easier to build, but it can only be used in the latitude for which the hour markings around its face have been calculated. In any other latitude it won't show the right time.

The biggest drawback of the sundial was that it was useless during cloudy weather or at night, so the next timekeepers to be invented didn't depend upon the sun at all. These were the clepsydras, or water clocks, of the Egyptians and Greeks, the sand clocks and those that told the time by the burning of a cord or candle or of a vessel filled with oil.

Water clocks worked on the basis of a jar with the hours painted on a scale inside it, from which water dripped from a tiny hole in its bottom. As the water level fell it sank past the hour markings and so told the time.

Of course somebody had to be on hand to fill the jar when it was empty. There was also another drawback — when the jar was full the pressure forced the water out of the hole faster than when it was nearly empty, so the first hours marked were shorter than the last. In later clepsydras this trouble was avoided by using two jars, the first one very large, in which the pressure remained constant much longer. The water dripped into a smaller jar with a float which marked the hours as it rose. The big jar could be filled as often as desired without disturbing the float. In some water clocks the small jar tipped over and emptied itself when it was full, then swung back into place ready for another filling.

There were hundreds of variations in the design of water clocks. Some had wheels with cups in their rims, like mill wheels. When a cup filled it turned the wheel a little and a pointer or hand fixed to its axle told the time on the dial.

A very simple burning clock was merely a piece of cord with knots tied in it, evenly spaced. One end was set afire and the rope smoldered slowly, consuming one marked knot after another. Candle clocks too were very simple. Candles of a certain size were marked with the hours, after testing to see how fast they would burn down. In lamp clocks the oil was poured into a glass reservoir graduated to mark the hours. As the lamp burned the level of the oil sank slowly down the scale, just as with a water clock.

Sand clocks or hourglasses were glass cylinders shaped like a dumbbell, with a hole in the slender center neck which joined them. The hole was just large enough for a tiny trickle of sand to fill the empty bottom cylinder in an hour. To use the hourglass you simply upended it, which put the filled half on top. When it was empty one hour had passed and you turned it over again.

All these clocks had a common fault — somebody had to be around every time they needed filling or upending. Neither they nor the sundials kept *continuous* time. At last the mechanical clock appeared on the scene. By the thirteenth century, clocks were fairly common in Europe, most of them large tower clocks.

At first they had neither faces nor hands. They simply struck bells for the hours; in fact, the word "clock" comes from the French word *cloche,* meaning "bell."

After a while the face or dial was added, with a single revolving hour hand to tell the time between bells. Much later the minute hand was introduced to give still closer time.

All the very early clocks were weight-driven. A long rope or chain with a heavy weight fastened to one end was wound round and round a drum. Then the dangling weight tugging at the rope made the drum revolve until the rope was all unwound. Then the clock would stop unless somebody cranked up the drum and wound the rope around it again.

Power from the revolving drum was transferred by cogwheels to the axles on which the clock hands were mounted and made them turn. Of course you can see that without some kind of regulator the weight rope would unwind in a few minutes and stop the clock. This regulator, the "heart" of the clock movement, is called the "escapement."

The earliest escapement we know anything about was called the "foliot balance." The first time we hear of it was when King Charles V of France ordered a Dutchman named Henry de Vick to build a clock for the Royal Palace in Paris, and de Vick installed a clock with a foliot balance there in 1364.

The idea behind all escapements is the same.

The drum which is being turned by the weight has a set of gear teeth around it. The balance, which swings

from side to side or up and down, has a stop or pallet at either end. One pallet drops between two teeth of the drum gear and stops it for an instant. Then the curved side of the tooth pushes the pallet up and releases the drum. As it starts to move, the balance arm forces the pallet at the other end of it between two other teeth of the drum and stops it again. Thus the drum is alternately stopped and released, which causes the tick-tock noise of all clocks, and the drum's turning speed is controlled.

You can see by the drawing how the pallets engage

the teeth of the escape wheel in the drawing of the foliot balance. This escapement had one bad feature, though. When the pallet was forced down between the gear teeth, it pushed the wheel back a little each time. This push, repeated thousands of times, caused the teeth to wear, and presently the clock no longer kept good time.

Then in 1675 Dr. Robert Hooke, an Englishman, invented the anchor escapement, a big improvement over the foliot balance, soon to be followed by a still better one called the "anchor deadbeat." This was designed so that when the pallets engaged the teeth they didn't back the wheel, and so caused much less wear.

For a long time all clocks were weight-driven, and a lot of room was needed below them to allow the weights to drop. Then in 1581 an idea for a different kind of clock was born in Pisa, Italy. One day the famous sixteenth-century scientist Galileo was idly watching a hanging lamp suspended from chains, swinging in a draft.

His brilliant mind was suddenly alerted to something nobody else had ever noticed. As the swinging lamp slowed down he noticed that it took the lamp just as long to complete a small swing as it did a much longer one. Galileo checked this odd fact again and again by timing the swings with his own pulsebeats which he counted with the finger tips of one hand on his other wrist. He had discovered the principle of the pendulum, isochronism, meaning "unequal arcs in equal time."

Galileo never made use of his discovery, but other men did. About 1665 Christian Huygens, a Dutch astronomer, and Dr. Hooke, the Englishman who had invented the anchor escapement, each designed a clock driven by coiled steel springs instead of by weights, and controlled the unwinding of the springs by an escapement worked by a pendulum. They knew this would be reliable because of Galileo's discovery of the principle of isochronism.

The pendulum had one fault. Because iron expands and contracts with changes of temperature, the length of the pendulum could change and so change the speed of the arcs and also the clock hands. Two improvements took care of this. One was the grid pendulum, made of alternating bars of brass and iron instead of one iron rod. Because iron and brass react differently to changes in temperature the expansion was equalized. The other method was to use a tube filled with mercury instead of the usual brass disc as the pendulum weight. The rise and fall of the mercury in the tube as the temperature changed (as in a thermometer) offset the expansion of the iron rod.

Strange and Wonderful Clocks of the Past

From earliest days clockmakers have been fascinated by the challenge of making clocks do many other things besides telling the hours. Some clock dials showed the days, months and years, the phases of the moon and stars, and the equinoxes. Others displayed clockwork figures which came out of doorways at certain hours, bowed, danced, played fiddles, blew horns and then disappeared. There were clocks which put on complete puppet shows every quarter hour. Some had birds that moved their wings and sang, donkeys that kicked, knights on horseback, and religious processions.

Medieval clocksmiths especially loved to design

clocks with odd ways of striking the hours. They built figures of every sort, aproned blacksmiths who swung great hammers against bells, woodchoppers who struck them with axes, turbaned Moors, even bears and lions. These figures were so common that they had a special name, "jack-o'-the-clocks," or in French, *jacquemarts*.

Artisans in the Black Forest in Germany developed a little clock which looked like a small cottage buried among leafy branches. From a tiny door above the clock face, which swung open on the hour, out popped

a little wooden bird which flapped its wings and called "cuckoo, cuckoo," as many times as the hour called for.

Clocks were made of every sort of material, wood, brass, iron, jade, ebony, porcelain, and many others. In Russia enameled and bejeweled clocks were made in the shape of Easter eggs. Some rather odd craftsmen even built clocks entirely of matches. Gardeners designed flower beds to keep time — they were living sundials.

One of the most interesting and elaborate of the ancient clocks was the triple-towered three-story-high astronomical clock in a special room in the rear of the beautiful Strasbourg cathedral in Alsace, France. This marvelous creation had a celestial globe, showing the position of the sun, moon and stars, a perpetual calendar and many moving processions and single figures, including a procession of the pagan gods for whom the days of the week were named. At the summit of this remarkable clock stands a proud rooster, designed to ruffle its feathers, flap its wings and crow three times.

Twice a day, at noon and midnight, the clock comes to life and all the figures perform. Each noon, to this day, tourists and townspeople crowd into the room until there is hardly space to breathe, to watch the performance.

All Strasbourg children have been brought up on a

legend about the old clock, now over 600 years old. The story is that the German king who had ordered the clock to be built in 1352 was so delighted with it that he wanted it to be the only one of its kind. He began to fear that its designer might create an even more wonderful clock for some other royal patron, so he simply ordered the man to be blinded.

Years passed, and one day the great clock stopped. None of the local clocksmiths could repair the complicated machinery completely, so at last the king sent for the blinded designer and asked him whether he could repair the clock without his eyesight. The old man agreed to try and climbed slowly inside the clock among the wheels and gears and set to work — not to repair it but to gain a long-delayed revenge by wrecking it completely.

For a long time the great clock stood silent. Then, many years later, a master clocksmith was found who was able to put it all back in working order — all, that is, except for the rooster at the summit. He could never be made to crow again.

4. Time At Sea

NOW we come to the most important clock in history. It has saved more lives and property and affected the lives of more people than any other clock ever did. This was the nautical chronometer.

Ever since men started voyaging out of sight of land, astronomers and mathematicians had been trying to find ways by which a shipmaster could fix his position on the ocean when his ship was out of sight of land. The compass could tell him the direction of magnetic north, so he knew which way his ship's bow was pointing. Yet, if he drew a straight line on his chart from home port to destination and steered his ship by a compass course which followed that line, he would soon be many miles off his course. This was because of winds and currents that made the hull drift sideways, and for which even the best helmsman couldn't compensate.

Something had to be found from which to take bearings when there was no land in sight. This left only the sun, moon and stars. Astronomers had discovered that these heavenly bodies followed a regular pattern in their orbits and they had worked out tables showing their altitudes at every hour of the day or night. By using these angles they could locate any place on earth very accurately. Now they had to discover a way to do the same thing at sea.

We have learned about the tables giving the sun's declination, which gave its position in degrees north or south of the equator for every day of the year. By sighting the sun along his backstaff or octant (early forms of the sextant, an instrument to measure in degrees how far above the horizon the sun is seen) at noon, he could read on its scale the sun's altitude from his ship's position. Then he looked up the sun's declination for that day which told him how far north or south of the equator the sun was. By adding or subtracting this distance (depending on whether the sun was on his side or the opposite side of the equator) he got a result which showed how far north or south of the equator his ship was.

In the illustrated diagram the navigator's backstaff

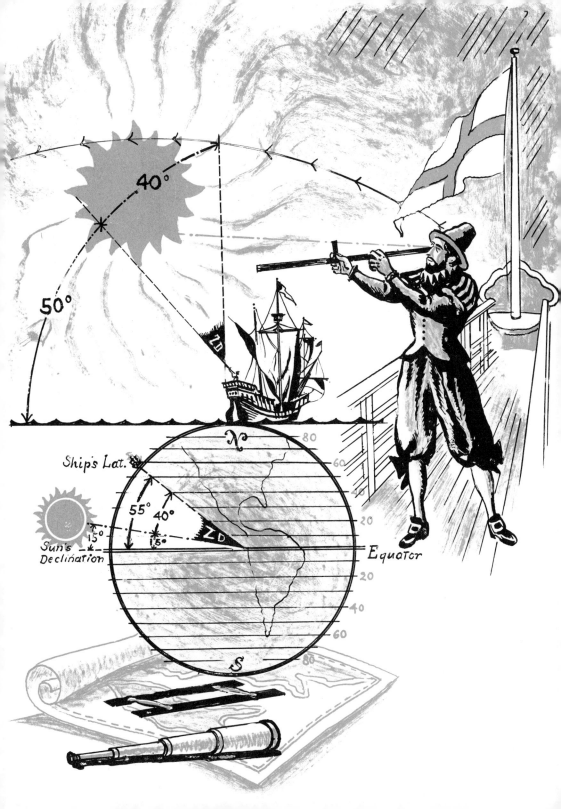

40°

50°

Ship's Lat.

55° 40°

Sun's
Declination

15° 15°

N

80

60

40

20

Z.D.

Equator

20

40

60

S

80

shows the sun's latitude to be 50 degrees. Subtracted from the 90-degree right angle formed between horizon and zenith, there remains a 40-degree angle, called ZD (zenith distance). For navigating use, angle ZD is the same as ZD^1, formed between a line running from the center of the earth to the zenith and another from the center of the earth to the sun.

The nautical almanac shows the sun's declination for that day to be 15 degrees, north latitude; by adding the ZD angle of 40 degrees to the 15 degrees declination, the total is 55 degrees, north latitude. This is the ship's position.

This was fine as far as it went but these observations gave the poor navigator not the slightest idea *where* on that line of latitude his ship lay; he could have been in the Atlantic, the Pacific, or in a lake somewhere in Asia.

This was all the help Columbus and the other early explorers got from the sky. With the aid of the compass and the ship's log, which told them roughly their speed over the water, they plotted their course by what was called "dead reckoning," which was often a long way from dead right. Each noon, weather permitting, they "shot the sun" for their latitude, until they reached the parallel on which their port lay. Then they turned and sailed along it until they sighted land — providing they had turned in the right direction.

Naturally a course that followed two legs of a triangle wasn't the quickest way of reaching a destination, so many of the more intelligent navigators were eager for some way of finding their longitude, or east-west position on the surface of the globe.

This was terribly important to the great seafaring nations, England, Holland, Spain, and Portugal especially, and they offered rich prizes to anyone who could solve the problem. Meanwhile, Galileo, who had discovered the first four satellites of Jupiter, put together a timetable of their eclipses as they circled around the planet, which covered 24 years. With this timetable he declared it would be possible to calculate the longitude of any place on earth. His plan was rejected by the scientists of that day but it was later remembered and used successfully in the 1670's by the French Académie, when that body was making the first modernization of the map of the world since the time of Claudius Ptolemy in Egypt in 150 A.D.

The new map located the seacoasts of the world on their proper longitude and latitude. Finding longitude at sea was still beyond reach, but the astronomers had worked out a celestial timetable called the Nautical Almanac by which a navigator could tell when the sun would cross any meridian of longitude, figured from the time at Greenwich, England.

For example, the navigator of a ship at sea would

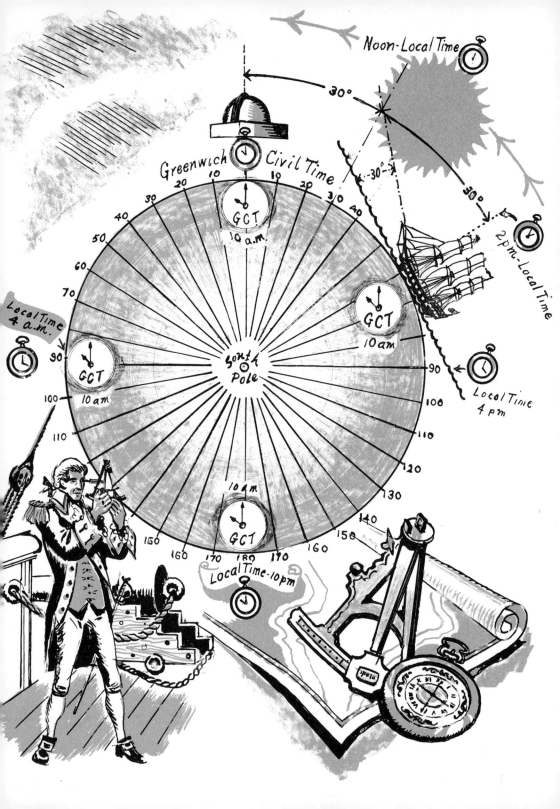

take a sight of the sun, as illustrated in the Longitude diagram, toward the end of the afternoon. The angle obtained, as read from his sextant, showed the ship's zenith (the point directly overhead in the sky) to be 30 degrees from the meridian over which the sun was passing at that instant. Now if only he had a clock aboard set to agree with Greenwich or 0 longitude time exactly, he could tell by referring to his almanac that the sun was then 30 degrees from 0 longitude at that instant.

By adding these 30 degrees to the 30 degrees his ship was east of the sun, he would get a sum of 60 degrees, east longitude, the ship's east-west position.

A degree of longitude at the equator equals 68 miles or four minutes in time. If a navigator on a six-week voyage expected to fix his position within half a degree or thirty-four miles, his clock must not gain or lose more than 2 minutes during the whole voyage, or 3 seconds a day. A greater error might put his ship on the rocks.

So far only the great pendulum clocks in the observatories could keep such close time, but the rolling of a ship would interfere with the arcs of a pendulum clock. No clockmaker had ever dreamed of building a timepiece which could keep such accurate time on a ship.

England was then in her time of greatest glory and Britain's boast that the sun never set on the Union Jack was coming true, but her power rested on her shipping. British frigates and merchantmen ranged to the far corners of the earth, to the Indies, the Americas, even to the fog-shrouded North Pacific. All too often ships were marked "overdue" for many months and finally written off as "lost at sea" with no hint of their final tragedies. The toll of disasters at sea, often due to faulty navigation, grew so heavy that finally the government had to take some action.

Parliament offered rich prizes to inventors to encourage them to tackle the job of building an accurate chronometer. In 1714 it passed a bill offering 10,000 pounds sterling for any device determining longitude within one degree, 15,000 pounds within 40 minutes, and 20,000 pounds for a fix as close as 30 minutes longitude (34 sea miles).

It also organized a permanent Board of Longitude to take charge of the contest, judge all inventions submitted and grant smaller prizes for promising work, even if it fell short of fulfilling the requirements.

Then for over 50 years all sorts of devices were submitted, but none of them worked, and the Board and the "crazy" inventors became the butt of jokes and comic rhymes. The prizes lay unclaimed.

Twenty-one years before the prize offer was made, a son was born to a carpenter in Foulby, Yorkshire.

The boy was named John Harrison, and by the time he was six years old, like many small boys today, he was taking things apart. The difference was that when John took a watch apart he put it back together so that it ran better than it had before.

He had such a genius for mechanics that by the time he was twenty-two he had built a grandfather's clock with hand-carved wheels and gears. Soon afterward he invented the grid clock pendulum, described earlier, and a new type of escapement called a "grasshopper escapement" which was better than anything before it.

His inquiring mind must have been challenged by that fabulous 20,000-pound prize which caused excitement all over Europe at a time when a man had to work hard all day for only a few pennies. Yet it was 14 years before he set out for London to show the Board his grid pendulum and grasshopper escapement. There he met Edmund Halley, Astronomer Royal, the discoverer of Halley's Comet, who persuaded the young man to go home and build a clock designed to win the big prize, instead of trying for a small grant.

Harrison went back to his shop and struggled for seven years to perfect a set of works which would run perfectly in the cabin of a pitching ship in any kind of

weather. At last he was satisfied that he had a clock that would do the job, although it was big and clumsy and weighed 72 pounds.

A year dragged by before the Royal Society approved it and the slow-moving Board of Longitude arranged for Harrison to put his clock aboard a warship for a sea trial on a cruise to Lisbon. We don't know what happened on the outbound voyage, but as H.M.S. *Orford* approached England on the return trip, her commander, Captain Man, entered this notation in his official ship's log:

> When we made land, the said land, according to my reckoning and others, ought to have been the Start, (a river) but before we knew what the land was, John Harrison declared to me and to the rest of the ship's company, that according to his observations with his machine, it ought to be the Lizard (a point of land) the which it indeed was found out to be, his observation showing the ship to be more west than by my reckoning, above one degree and 26 miles.

Here was a frank admission by one of His Majesty's Royal Naval Captains that his own calculations were 90 miles off in such familiar waters as the Channel approaches. It paints a gloomy picture of the state of the art of navigation before the marine chronometer.

Harrison was awarded 500 pounds by the Board

after they heard Captain Man's testimony; this money was to be used by Harrison to build a second and, if possible, a smaller chronometer. In 1739 he completed his second clock, and while it was an improvement over No. 1, it was even larger, weighing 102 pounds. This was tested for two years but was never sent on a voyage, because the war with Spain made the Admiralty hesitate to risk its capture by the Dons.

Harrison was given another 500 pounds to keep him from starvation while he built a third clock, which he tinkered with for five years. Reluctantly at the age of sixty-four, he decided that No. 3 would never work and scrapped the whole thing. No. 4 was a complete departure from its big, cumbersome predecessors. It was shaped like a large thick watch, only about five inches in diameter, and instead of suspending it from gimbals like the others he fitted it into a plain wooden box, like the modern chronometer. It was a beautifully constructed piece of mechanism, jeweled to the third wheel with rubies, with diamonds for the end stones. John Harrison thanked God that he had been spared long enough to complete "this my Watch or Time-keeper for the Longitude, than which there is no other mechanical or mathematical thing in the world that is more beautiful or curious in texture."

After two more years of testing, the Board decided

to give the new chronometer a sea trial aboard H.M.S. *Deptford*, Captain Dudley Digges, on a voyage to Jamaica. By now Harrison was sixty-eight years old and in such poor health that he was unable to withstand the rigors of a winter voyage on a sailing vessel. His son William, whom he had trained, took his place aboard the *Deptford*, which sailed from Spithead with a convoy on November 18, 1761.

The Lords of the Admiralty were a slow-moving body in eighteenth-century Britain. They were very suspicious of anything new, and the post captains under them felt the same way. Captain Digges and his officers were no exception. They treated Harrison's newfangled watch with polite disbelief.

To prevent any trickery, the chronometer was secured in a strongbox with four locks, one key being held by Governor Lyttleton of Jamaica, who was returning to his post, one by young Harrison, one by Captain Digges, and one by his first lieutenant. Unless all four keys were present the clock could not be unlocked to be wound or adjusted in any way.

Young Harrison plotted the ship's course daily, using the captain's observations and his father's chronometer, to the scornful smiles of the officers, who were plotting the course in the old-fashioned way. Then nine days out of Spithead it was found that the beer aboard had spoiled and all hands were deprived of their daily ration.

The captain changed course to make for the island of Madeira, where they could buy more beer, but in those days it was easy to overrun such a small island. As they neared it the captain pored over his chart and set a double lookout. His dead reckoning put them 13 degrees 50 minutes west of Greenwich. Here young Harrison spoke up and insisted that by *his* reckoning they were 15 degrees 19 minutes west, and that they would sight Madeira next morning. Here was a pretty situation — the skill and honor of the British navy was being doubted, and by a landlubber! Captain Digges scornfully offered to bet Harrison he was wrong at odds of 5 to 1.

The captain would have lost his bet; at six o'clock the next morning the cry of "Land ho, dead ahead" rose from the lookout in the crosstrees. Porto Santo, one of the Madeira group, lay on the horizon.

When the ship reached Jamaica, the box was taken ashore, opened, and the chronometer solemnly inspected. The watch was found to be only five seconds slow for the whole voyage, an error of only 1¼ nautical miles. This was far better than it needed to be to win the big prize!

Young Harrison embarked on the return voyage

with a full heart, which was soon offset by an emptied stomach, because the weather turned very rough during the whole trip, and the chronometer was given a rigorous testing in the pitching, rolling ship. Nevertheless, when it was checked at Portsmouth at the end of the voyage its total error for the five-month period was only 1 minute 53½ seconds, amounting to only 28½ minutes of longitude. This performance more than met the conditions of the contest, and so John Harrison confidently applied for the 20,000-pound prize which he so richly deserved after almost a lifetime of work.

Instead he ran into one delay and evasion after another. Jealous fellow competitors in the Royal Society had spent large sums on their own experiments and they used every ounce of their influence to hold up payment, hoping for a try at it themselves. Finally the Board declared that the chronometer's performance might have been a fluke and demanded further tests. Meanwhile they doled out a temporary award of only 2,500 pounds while Parliament voted him 5,000 pounds if he would reveal the secret of his watch — which he indignantly refused to do.

Finally Chronometer No. 4 was put aboard H.M.S. *Tartar* along with its faithful attendant, William, on a voyage to Barbados for yet another test. Once again, on the return to Portsmouth, the watch was checked and found to have gained only 54 seconds in 156 days.

Again the Board hedged. While they had to admit that Harrison's chronometer had kept the longitude well within the limits of the contest, they refused to pay him the balance of the first 10,000 pounds until he had submitted complete working drawings of No. 4, shown the Board how each part was made and operated, and turned over all four of his clocks to them.

He was bitterly disappointed and almost lost hope, but his friends raised such a clamor that the public became interested and forced the Board to pay him the first half of the prize. A hard fight still lay ahead before he was able to pry the second half out of them.

Harrison was now forced to take his clock apart and demonstrate it before the Board, which then took charge of it in trust, for the benefit of all the people of England. Almost at once, though, somebody was able to copy the plans and publish them without his permission. Meanwhile all sorts of tests were made by various horologists, to try to discredit it if possible. Finally Harrison was ordered to build two more clocks which were to go through more tests before the Board would release the rest of the prize.

Harrison, by now seventy-eight years old, slowly going blind and with unsteady hands, was desperate. He complained that he had scarcely been paid a laborer's wages for the long years he had toiled to perfect his chronometers. He appealed directly to King George III, who had met him and admired his skill and perseverance. The king, angered by the long delays and unfair demands of the Board of Longitude, threatened to appear before the Bar of Commons himself to argue the case. That did the trick. The combination of royal favor and the threat of action by Commons caved in their resistance. Parliament at once passed a money bill, the king signed it, and at last Harrison had his prize money in full.

5. The Clockmakers and Their Guild

THE early clockmakers made each part of a clock entirely by hand, using only the simplest tools — hammer, drill, saw and file. Only later did they have foot-power lathes. The wheels and pinions were usually made of brass, which they themselves made by melting copper and zinc together. The brass was poured into sand molds to make rough castings of the gears and wheels, which they then had to polish and file until each part fitted. The brass castings were often too soft to work, so they had to be tempered or hardened by "planishing," hammering them lightly hour after hour under water. This must have been a shivery job for an apprentice boy on a cold winter day.

Up to the nineteenth century, clocks were usually made only to order, no two of them were alike and parts made for one clock wouldn't fit another. They were made in small shops, each run by a master clockmaker with two journeymen or helpers. There were usually several apprentices, boys of from nine years upward, whose parents signed them over to the master to learn the clockmaking trade. They were bound for from four to seven years without pay, before becoming journeymen.

The English clockmakers were organized into a guild, the union of the seventeenth century, except that the owners were members instead of the workmen. The guild, called the Worshipful Clock Makers' Company, was very powerful. It even had its own coat of arms. It limited the number of journeymen in each shop to two, set the wages and working hours of the workmen, and the number of clocks the shop might make each month. It even set the prices. These regulations were to prevent any master from becoming a Henry Ford of the clock world and so putting other makers out of business. The guild inspected the work of each shop from time to time; if a clock was found to be below guild standards it was destroyed and the shop owner fined heavily.

English clockmakers came to the American colonies, along with silversmiths, cabinetmakers and other skilled craftsmen, as soon as the small settlements grew into towns. The most famous of the early masters was Eli Terry, who began as an apprentice in 1768. By 1800 Terry, now a skilled craftsman, set up shop for himself at Plymouth, near Waterbury, Connecticut. At this time it was difficult to get brass, which had to be shipped over from England and so was not only scarce but expensive. For this reason American clock-makers built the works of their clocks almost entirely of hardwood, carving the delicate teeth in wheels made of maple or some other durable wood. It was slow, painstaking work, and it took many hours of labor to put together one clock, so of course the prices had to be rather high. Most masters were afraid to risk making clocks on speculation. They usually preferred to wait until somebody came into the shop and ordered one before they set to work.

Terry decided this was too slow a way of doing business. He felt sure that a great many people needed clocks and would buy them if someone showed them one, so he became one of the earliest traveling salesmen. With four or five of his wooden-works clocks packed carefully in his saddlebags, he rode along the back-country roads of Connecticut looking for business.

He would stop at every likely-looking farmhouse and unpack his clocks, but often the farmer complained that the prices were too high. Terry had to

charge from $20 to $40, which was a lot of money in those days, when a laborer worked 12 or 14 hours for 50 cents. Clever Eli would then ask permission to leave a clock at the farmhouse and pick it up on his way back. By the time he returned the family had come to depend so much on their new timepiece that they couldn't do without it.

One day he got a contract from a merchant to make 4,000 wooden-works clocks at $4 apiece. To fill such an order he needed help and so he took in as partner a young carpenter named Seth Thomas. This was the beginning of the famous firm of Terry & Thomas which, over the years, made some of the most beautiful American clocks, such as the popular broken-arch and the pillar and scroll models.

In 1808 Seth Thomas and a man named Hoadley bought out Eli Terry and began a company which is still making clocks in the Connecticut valley. About this time Simon Willard of Grafton, Massachusetts, designed and started making the famous and beautiful "banjo" wall clock. Because of its length Willard was able to use a weight instead of a spring for power, and a longer pendulum to regulate the escapement. He claimed that his banjo model was more accurate than any other wall clock.

By the 1820's clocks were being made of brass instead of wood, and more and more machinery was being used to turn them out. At that time clock movements were often used in barter; horses were sometimes sold for so many clock movements instead of dollars.

Because the new machines could turn out clock parts which were all exactly alike, it was now possible

to use assembly-line methods to build clocks much cheaper than by the old one-at-a-time hand way. Prices came down steadily until by 1840 the factory of Chauncey Jerome, at Bristol, Rhode Island, turned out good clocks for only $5. This was an unheard-of price anywhere but in America; European clocks were still being made by hand.

Jerome decided to try selling his clocks in England. He sent a salesman with the wonderful name of Epaphroditus Peck to England with several cases of his clocks, but on landing Peck ran afoul of the British customs officers. They didn't believe that the valuation of $5 he put on his clocks was honest, because they thought nobody could build a clock so cheaply. They felt sure he was undervaluing his wares to save duty, and decided to teach him a lesson. British law permitted the customs officers to seize any merchandise they suspected of being undervalued, by paying the owner *his* declared value plus 10 percent. So Mr. Peck got $5.50 for each clock without even having to remove the cases from the dock or to pay *any* duty. The customs men thought they had a bargain and Peck got 50 cents more for each clock than he had hoped to sell them for. Jerome was delighted and at once began shipping clocks by the thousand to England and happily collecting his 10 percent profit from the British

Customs. It was too good to last; the Customs soon saw they had a bear by the tail, and allowed Peck to bring in his clocks at his own valuation.

By 1875 the circular alarm clock with a bell on top came out, and reproductions of the beautiful old Colonial models, as well, unfortunately, as a lot of very ugly designs, were being turned out at prices which anybody could afford.

The final step came in 1914, when Henry Warren of Ashford, Massachusetts, developed a small electric motor which would run a clock with wonderful accuracy — and *never* had to be wound! Today almost all large clocks and many smaller ones are run by motors.

Modern designers have done remarkable things with the clock face. Modern clocks often don't even look like clocks. Instead of the usual circle of numbers some modern clocks just have a circle of small brass knobs or discs on a room wall, with the hands projecting from the center of the circle. Others are mounted on sheets of plate glass or in transparent globes. You can buy one to harmonize with a room in which George Washington would have felt at home, or with an exciting modern interior with picture windows, indirect lighting and furniture made of glass and metal. Classical or modern, they have one thing in common — they all keep accurate time.

6. The Story of Watches

BEFORE the sixteenth century people must have looked wistfully at the great tower clocks that boomed the hours, and wished for some magic way of telling time when they were out of sight and hearing of the clock towers. If only there were some way of making a clock small enough to carry around by a strap or handle, or even, wildly foolish idea that it was, for a timepiece that could be carried in the *pocket*.

Now a Peter Henlein of Nuremberg makes his bow in the history of timekeeping. It is the year 1500. Peter was a clockmaker who didn't think that the idea of a portable clock was too fantastic; he was determined to design a lightweight small clock which kept good time and could be carried around. Of course you couldn't use weights or pendulums — they would drag on the ground. So he used a spring made of a strip of flexible steel, which could be wound up around a post by means of a key. As it unwound it would supply the power to run the works.

Henlein's "carrying-clock" was massive and its iron wheels and cogs took up so much room that the case had to be very thick. In fact it was nicknamed "the Nuremberg Egg" because it was as thick as it was round. Alas, it failed to keep good time because its designer hadn't worked out a dependable device to take the place of a pendulum to balance his mainspring. Also, as the spring ran down it lost power and the watch began to lose time.

Now we hear once more from Dr. Robert Hooke, inventor of the anchor escapement. He used a hair or bristle from a hog's hide, which was so tough it would bend and snap back over and over, without breaking, to act as a regulator. Later the hog bristle was replaced by a steel spring, which has always been called a "hairspring."

There was still the problem of the watch slowing down as the spring unwound. A weird contrivance of arms, cams and gears, called the "stockfreed," was invented to overcome the trouble but was not very successful. Then something new called a "fusee" was tried. This was a cone-shaped drum with a spiral groove cut

into it, around which was wound a cord or chain, running to the spring drum. As the spring unwound and the drum slowed, the cord to the fusee also slowed, but the higher the cord unwound from the narrowing cone, the faster it turned the fusee, which thus always turned at the same speed although the drum was slowing down.

The fusee remained a part of all watches for a long time, until a watchmaker named Abraham Breguet improved the hairspring by carrying the outer coil across the other coils and fastening it to the center of the spring. This equalized the pull of the spring and made possible a lighter, less stiff spring that only partly unwound before it was time to rewind the watch. This avoided the usual slowing down. All watchmakers except the British abandoned the fusee and so were able to make thinner watches which people preferred.

Not until 1550 did watchmakers stop using iron and turned to brass wheels and screws. By 1600 they were putting glass crystals over the watch faces. Minute hands were seldom used until 1700 because until then watches were so inaccurate that a minute hand would have been useless. In those days if you wanted to make sure of having the right time you carried two, or even three, watches to check against each other.

People thought of watches more as decorative jewelry than as timepieces, and makers spent most of their efforts in the decorations. Watches were set into beautifully carved rings, lockets, crosses and pendants, often set with precious stones. Ordinary people couldn't afford watches; only the rich wore them.

By the beginning of the eighteenth century the watchmakers were learning how to turn out accurate timepieces. In 1704 Nicholas Facio, a Swiss, introduced jeweled bearings in watches. Not everybody knows what a jeweler means when he talks of a 7-jewel or a 21-jewel watch. He's not referring to diamonds or pearls set into a design in the case to beautify the watch. In fact the jewels he's talking about are not even meant to be seen. They are tiny sapphires or rubies or other very hard jewels with tiny holes bored into them to form the bearings in which the delicate axles of the various wheels revolve.

In cheap watches these axles turn in tiny holes in brass bearings. After a few years the constant wear of metal against metal enlarges the hole and wears down the axle. Then the wheels begin to wobble and the watch stops keeping good time. Jeweled bearings are so hard and smooth that the wheels will turn for a lifetime without any wear. The more jeweled bearings there are in a watch the longer it will last.

If there is an old watch at home, one that might

have belonged to your great-grandfather, you may have noticed a tiny key dangling from the fob or chain. If so, you are looking at a key-winder. Early watches all had to be wound by opening the back of the case and inserting the watch key into a small hole. Not until late in the nineteenth century was stem-winding introduced.

Back in the gay nineties the proudest gift a boy could expect as a graduation present was a gold hunting-case watch. It had a hinged lid over the dial which had to be snapped open to see the watch face. It got its name because fox hunters who rode to hounds in Merrie England often fell off their horses after taking a fence or hedge. They needed watches with lids to protect the crystals from being smashed.

Both front and back lids were decorated with elaborate designs, with pictures of railroad locomotives, elks' heads, ships under sail, or hunting dogs, and owner's name or initials were engraved in a scrollwork design called "engine turning." Many watches, especially those for ladies to wear pinned to their blouses and called "chatelaines," even had small diamonds, rubies, emeralds and pearls set into the design.

The old hunting-case watches, which one seldom sees today, were solid and heavy, over half an inch thick, and made to last. It wasn't unusual for a father

to leave his son the watch he had inherited from his own father. Any young man who owned a solid-gold, hunting-case watch hung from a watered-silk fob with a gold-mounted elk's tooth, or from a massive gold chain with a couple of seals, was really sitting on top of the world. There was only one more peak to scale, to own a repeater watch.

Before the day of the luminous dial there was only one way to tell the time in the dark — that was to own a repeater, king of watches. Then all you had to do was to press a tiny lever on the case to make a silvery chime sound the hour in the darkness. Some repeaters even sounded the nearest quarter hour in a different tone.

World War I was responsible for the two latest changes in watch fashions. Before that hunting cases had gone out of style and pocket watches were getting thinner and thinner as the makers found new ways of arranging the wheels in the works. Still, almost every man carried his watch in his pocket. He'd sooner have gone out without his pants than be seen wearing a wrist watch, which was considered sissy.

The war soon changed that; soldiers found the wrist watch a must in the trenches, because they couldn't get at a pocket watch buried under overcoat, gas mask and cartridge belt. After the war the veterans refused to give up the handy wrist watch, now respectable and manly.

The war also brought the desperate need for a watch face which could be read in the dark. Repeaters cost too much and couldn't be heard during a barrage anyhow. Watchmakers then found that dial numbers and hands painted with radium paint would glow in the dark. With such a dial an infantry commander could tell when to blow his whistle for going over the top without lighting a match to look at his watch and being drilled by a sniper.

Although watches are made in many countries, the leader among all the nations is tiny Switzerland. The Swiss started early and have used every new method that has been discovered. Whole villages do nothing but make certain watch parts, which are then shipped to other towns where everybody assembles movements. So they are able to sell good watches cheaper than almost anybody else, and they export them all over the world.

American watch companies have been making good watches for a long time, as good as any. In 1850 Waltham was already in business, and for many years, Waltham, Hamilton, and Elgin have made watches for railroad men and others who have to have time-pieces which don't vary more than a couple of seconds a week.

The big problem in the early days was to turn out a cheap watch which would keep fairly good time. There was a big market waiting for such a watch; it was a challenge to the American genius for mass production.

Probably the first try was by a John Hopkins, who built a watch to sell for only 50 cents. Either the price didn't leave him any profit or the watch wasn't even worth 50 cents; Mr. Hopkins was soon out of business.

The next try was a result of a visit by Mr. Edward A. Lock to the Philadelphia Centennial Exhibit in 1876. He was fascinated by a miniature steam engine he saw there, which ran perfectly although it was so tiny it could be hidden in the palm of one's hand.

Later Lock decided to build a cheap, reliable watch, and remembered the marvelous workmanship of the little engine. Its builder should be able to build a watch without any trouble. He looked the man up and found him in a little shop with the Centennial engine in the window.

The builder, Mr. D. A. Buch, agreed to try to build a good watch for Mr. Lock, which could be sold for $4. After several tries Mr. Buch produced a watch with several new features to cut the cost of manufacture. One was to use the frame of the movement itself as the drum to wind the spring around. Thus was launched the famous Waterbury watch.

It was an immediate hit, and sold like hot cakes, although the mainspring was 9 feet long and took so long to wind that jokes sprang up about Waterbury watch owners who had to get help to wind, when they were worn out. The Waterbury was a kind of 1880 watch-maker's version of Ford's "tin Lizzie."

This watch caught the attention of a man whose name was to become world-famous for putting a watch into the pocket of almost every man and boy. Robert H. Ingersoll at that time knew little about watches. He was running a successful mail-order business, and in 1892 he bought 1000 Waterburys for 85 cents each and sold them by mail for $1.

This was the beginning of the famous Ingersoll Dollar Watch. The big, rather clumsy Waterbury was more a pocket clock than a watch, so Ingersoll improved the design and manufactured it himself. Men who owned good watches used Ingersolls at work, or on fishing trips. No small boy's life was complete without a Dollar Watch ticking noisily in his pocket. Cases of them were shipped all over the world, even as trade goods with African and South Sea Island natives.

For over twenty-five years the Ingersoll led the field of cheap watches, until the wrist watch grew popular and rising costs forced the company to raise the famous $1 price tag.

Still, the dollar watch was an important step in bringing reasonably priced, accurate timepieces to almost everyone instead of only a few wealthy people. It is also an important part of this story of the measurement of time, without which our lives would be turned topsy-turvy from morning to bedtime.

Now, when you look up at the sky, remember what an important part the sun, moon and stars play in timekeeping and watch their orbits.

Go to a planetarium whenever you can and learn about the ever-changing wonders of our night skies. When you look at a calendar think of how many changes were made before our present accurate one was worked out. Whenever you glance at your wrist watch remember what a long, long road stretches back from it to that first crude sundial.

GLOSSARY

Clepsydra — The Greek and Egyptian water clock. As water dripped steadily through a small hole in the bottom of a jar, the time could be told by comparing the declining water level inside the jar to hour markings painted on the sides of the jar.

Declination of the sun — The distance of the sun north or south of the equator on any day of the year.

Equinox — The biannual passage of the sun directly above the equator. The vernal equinox occurs on March 21st of each year; the autumnal equinox, on September 21st.

Escapement — The mechanism in a watch or clock which regulates the speed at which the spring uncoils. It is the operation of the escapement which causes the "tick-tock" sound and which insures that each minute will be the same length.

Greenwich Time — The time established at the Observatory in Greenwich, England, by observing the movements of stars through a telescope. Greenwich Time is used as a standard in fixing time throughout the world.

International date line — An imaginary line drawn through the most remote areas of the Pacific Ocean. Astronomers decided, for convenience in fixing dates, that one day would end and the next begin when that line had been crossed.

Meridian — An imaginary line in the sky passing directly over the observer's head and cutting through the North and South Poles.

Sidereal year — The actual time it takes for the earth to complete a full revolution around the sun. The sidereal year is six hours and nine minutes longer than the calendar year, a discrepancy which is made up by the extra day in each leap year.

Solstice, summer and winter — June 21st and December 21st of each year. On these dates the earth reaches its greatest tilt to the south and north respectively during its annual revolution around the sun.

Sundial — One of the first timekeepers. In its early form, the sundial consisted of an upright shaft tilted to point at the North Star. From the shadow it cast on a flat surface, marked with lines representing the hours, the approximate time of day could be told.

Zenith — The point in the sky which is directly above any place or observer.

INDEX